Short Stories About Animals, For Little Children

SHORT STORIES ABOUT ANIMALS

SHORT STORIES ABOUT ANIMALS

THE ANIMALS AND THE MAN'S BOOT—*See page* 13.

SHORT STORIES ABOUT ANIMALS

FOR LITTLE CHILDREN

IN WORDS OF ONE SYLLABLE

ILLUSTRATED BY HARRISON WEIR

THE GOAT AND SHEEP—*Page* 66.

GRIFFITH & FARRAN

(SUCCESSORS TO NEWBERY AND HARRIS)

WEST CORNER ST PAUL'S CHURCHYARD, LONDON

NEW YORK: E. P. DUTTON & CO.

TO

THREE DEAR LITTLE CHILDREN

FAR OVER THE SEA

(GERTIE, HILDA, AND PATTY),

THIS LITTLE BOOK

IS

DEDICATED.

CONTENTS.

HERE the big brown Owl doth hoot:
Where the Cat lays soft, sure foot:
Where the Wren and Thrush do fly:
Where the Pig grunts in his sty:
Where the Horse, best loved of man,
And the Dog, who loves him, dwell;
Where the Cows, as mild Cows can,
Raise their heads, and ring their bell:
Where upon the wide, wide plain,
Soft white Sheep make bare their way:
Where the Duck leads forth her train;
And the shy brown Hare doth play:
Where the bold black Goat doth roam:
Where the wild Bird finds her home:
There, ere this your day be done,
Look, and learn, both Sire and Son.

Short Stories about Animals.

I.—"Of Course."

N a dark wood, where wild beasts lived, there once lay a man's boot. How it got there I can not say, for no man had been there; at least the beasts had not seen one in all their lives. But there the boot was, and when the beasts saw it, they all came round to find out what it was. Such a thing was quite new to them, but they were not much at a loss, for all that.

"Well, there is no doubt as to what it is, I say," said the Bear.

"Oh, of course not," said the Wolf, and the Goat, and all the beasts and birds, in one breath.

"Of course," said the Bear. "It is the rind of

some kind of fruit off a tree. The fruit of the cork, I should say. This is cork, it is plain to see;" and he shewed the sole of the boot.

"Oh! just hear him! just hear him!" cried all the beasts and birds.

"It's not that at all," said the Wolf, with a glance of scorn at the Bear. "Of course it is some kind of nest. Look! here is the hole for the bird to go in at, and here is the deep part for the eggs and young ones to be safe. No doubt at all, of course not."

"Oh! oh!" cried the Bear, and the Goat, and all the birds and beasts. "Just hear what he says. It is not that at all."

"I should think not," said the Goat. "It is quite a plain case. Look at this long root," and he shewed the lace at the side of the boot. "It is the root of a plant, of course."

"Not a bit of it," cried the Wolf and the Bear; "not a bit of it. A root! How can you say so? It is not that, we can all see."

"If I might speak," said an old Owl, who sat

in a tree near, "I think I can tell you what it is. I have been in a land where there are more of such things than you could count. It is a man's boot."

"A what?" cried all the beasts and birds. "What is a man? and what is a boot?"

"A man!" said the Owl. "Well, a Man is a thing with two legs, that can walk, and eat, and talk like us, but he can do much more than we can."

"Pooh! pooh!" cried they all.

"That can't be true!" said the beasts. "How can a thing with two legs do more than we can, who have four. It is false, of course."

"Of course it is, if they have no wings," said the birds.

"Well," went on the Owl, "they have no wings, and yet it is true. And they can make things like this, and they call them boots, and put them on their feet."

"Oh! oh!" cried all the beasts and birds at once. "How can you? For shame? Fie on you! That is not true, of course. It can not be."

"A fine tale!" said the Bear.

"Can do more than we can!" said the Wolf.

"Wear things on their feet!" said the Goat.

"Not true! not true!" cried they all. "On the face of it, your tale is not true. We know that such things are not worn on the feet. How could they be?"

"Of course they could not," said the Bear. "It is false."

"It must be false," cried all the birds and beasts. "You must leave the wood," they said to the Owl. "What you say can not be true. You are not fit to live with us. You have said what we know is false. It must be, of course."

And they chased the Owl out of the wood, and would not let him come back.

"It is true for all that," said the Owl. And so it was.

II.—"*By-and-Bye.*"

"WHEN shall you build your nest?" said a Thrush to a Jay, one fine day in the spring.

"Oh, by-and-bye, some time," said the Jay. "It is so fine now. I must hop, and fly, and sing, and have some fun, while I may."

"One can sing while one works," said the Thrush.

"When shall you build your nest?" asked the Jay.

"Mine? Oh! I have built some of it. Look!" and the Thrush, with a glad chirp, showed the bush where she had laid moss and twigs, and twined them so as to make part of a nest. "And now," said she, "I must be off to get some hay, or wool, or some more moss to go on with."

"Oh, come and have a bit of play," said the Jay. "Why don't you rest for a time?"

"Oh! that will come by-and-bye," said the Thrush. And she sang her song—

> "When I've done
> I'll have my fun;
> In my nest
> I'll take my rest;
> That I know will be the best."

"Well, well," said the Jay, "if you like to slave all the best part of your life, pray do."

"Of course," said the Thrush, "the best part of my life is to work in!"

"Time for work by-and-bye," said the Jay.

"Time for rest and play by-and-bye," said the Thrush. And off she flew, as she sang her short gay song.

"I don't like that song," said the Jay.

Day by day it was the same. The Thrush had built her nest, and laid five smooth, round eggs in it, and yet the Jay had not brought one stick to make hers. At last, one day, in great haste, she

THRUSH AND JAY.

brought some twigs, and some coarse grass, and laid them on a bough in a low bush. But she did not place them well, and when she had worked an hour or two, she left off, and went to see the Thrush, who sat on her nest in a bush close by.

"When will your nest be done?" said the Thrush.

"Oh, by-and-bye," said the Jay. "I must rest now. Have you found time to rest yet?"

"Oh dear no!" said the Thrush. "Just look, I have five dear little young ones here. How could I leave them, or find time to play? I fetch them food, or else sit here to keep them warm all day and all night. They are such dear wee things, and they do eat so much, the pets! I must be off now to get them some more food, I see! Time to rest by-and-bye, when they have grown up, and can get their own food." And off she flew.

The Jay's nest was not done, when one day she saw the Thrush with five young ones, all round her on the grass.

"Have you built your nest?" cried the Thrush.

"No," said the Jay. "At least, it is not done yet, but I have laid my eggs, and the rest of the nest I can build by-and-bye, when they are hatched."

"That won't do," thought the Thrush. But she did not say so.

That night came a great storm. It rocked the bush where the Jay had laid her eggs on the loose twigs and grass. They were not well twined, and there was no edge to keep the eggs safe. The eggs slipped on one side, and one by one they fell on the ground. When the Jay woke next day, all her eggs were gone, and bits of shell lay strewed on the ground round the bush.

And that was what came of the Jay's "By-and-bye."

III.—"*I'll Pay You Out.*"

NOW this is an odd tale, but if you do not think it is at all true, why that is a good thing.

A Hen trod on a Duck's foot. She did not mean to do it, and it did not hurt much, but the Duck would pay her out, she said. So she flew at the Hen, but as she did so, her wing struck a Cock, who stood close by.

"I'll pay you out," cried he, and he flew at the Duck. But as he did so, his claw tore the fur of a Cat, who was just then in the yard.

"I'll pay you out," cried she, and she flew at the Cock. But as she did so, her tail went in the eye of a Sheep who was near.

"I'll pay you out," cried he, and he ran at the Cat. But as he did so, his foot caught the foot of the Dog, who lay in the sun.

" I'll pay you out," cried he, and he ran at the Sheep. But as he did so, his leg struck an old Cow, who stood by the gate.

" I'll pay you out," cried she, and she ran at the Dog. But as she did so, her horn grazed the skin of a Horse, who was by a tree.

" I'll pay you out," cried he, and he ran at the Cow.

There was a run! The Horse flew at the Cow, and the Cow at the Dog, and the Dog at the Sheep, and the Sheep at the Cat, and the Cat at the Cock, and the Cock at the Duck, and the Duck at the Hen. What a noise they made, to be sure!

" What is all this?" said the man, who took care of them. " I can not have this noise." So he took a great stick. " You may stay here," he said to the Hen. But he drove the Cock to his roost, and the Duck to her pond, and the Cat to her hearth, and the Sheep to her fold, and the Dog to his house, and the Cow to her field, and the Horse to his stall. " I'll pay you all out," said he.

IV.—"*I Wish.*"

 DOG saw a cat on the top of a high wall. And he said, " I wish I could get up there. It must be so nice to sit up so high: but I can not climb." And he was cross, and would not wag his tail.

Then he went on, and saw a Bird in the air. And he said, "I wish I could fly like that Bird. What fun it must be! and I am so dull here." And he felt still more cross.

Then he came to a pond, and saw a Fish in it. And he said, "I wish I could live in a pond all the day. Then I should not be so hot as I am now." And he would not look at the Fish, but shut his eyes, and lay down on the grass.

Then he heard the Fish say, "Oh, I wish I could lie down on the fresh green grass, like that Dog! It does look so nice and warm out there."

The dog sat up, and went back by the road he had come.

As he went he saw the Bird, and he heard it say, "I wish I could play all day long like that dog, and have a house made for me to live in. I have to make a nest, and my wings are so tired; yet I must fly to and fro, day by day, till it is done."

Then he saw the Cat on the wall, and heard her say, "There goes that spoilt old Dog home to get his plate of meat! I wish I was as well off, and could get meat like him. I have had no food all this long day. I wish I was like that dog!"

DOG AND CAT.

V.—"*I Don't Care.*"

 SHALL go this way," said a young black Colt, who was out on the moor. And he looked down the road.

"No, no," said a Horse who was close by. "You must stop on the moor."

"Why?" asked the Colt.

"I can not tell," said the Horse, "I have been told to stay by an old Horse, and so I shall."

"I don't care," said the young Colt, and off he set down the road.

By-and-bye he met an old Mare, at an inn door. "What are you here for?" asked she.

"I have come out for a bit of fun," said the Colt.

"But you should not," said the Mare. "You are not fit to go out in the world. You have no shoes on."

"I don't care," said the Colt, and he kicked his heels high up in the air to show that he did not mind what the old Mare said. But the Mare was a Mare of few words, and she said no more.

Then he went on down the road, as fast as he could tear.

He met a Mule with a pack on his back. The Mule shook his head when he saw the Colt.

"You should not be here," he said. "You have come off the moor, I know. The town is close by."

"I don't care," said the Colt. And he tore on.

Right on through the town he went. He had not been in a town in all his life. And the noise, and the sight of all the men, and carts, and things, made him feel quite mad. He tore here, and he tore there, while men and boys ran to catch him, and threw stones and sticks, and cried out at him, all up and down the streets.

At last, in a great sheet of glass, he saw what he thought was a young Colt, and he ran up to ask it what he should do, and how he could get back to the moor. Of course, it was not a Colt, but his own self that he saw in the glass.

The glass cut him when he dashed at it, and he fell down. And then he was caught.

"Why, that is my young Colt off the moor!" said a man who just then came up. " These are his tricks, are they? He must have a great clog of wood tied to his feet, then."

So he was led back to the moor, with his head cut, and his feet all sore, and there he had to stump from spot to spot with a great clog tied to his feet. He did not say, "I don't care" then.

VI.—"*Not My Fault.*"

ONE day a Hare was on the top of a high hill. In mere play, for he was gay and young, he kicked a small stone down the hill. Then he ran off, to leap and bound through the wood.

As the small stone fell, it hit a large stone, which moved too, and rolled down as well. And this large stone, as it went on, struck a rock, which lay on the side of the hill. The rock was not firm, and a small thing could move it. The stone struck it just at the base, and the rock shook and moved, and at last fell from its place.

It fell in the midst of a deep stream, which ran through the fields, with a bank on each side.

There the rock stood, in the midst of the stream. Day by day, the mud and sticks, that came down with the stream, were stopped by the rock, till they made quite a high bank. At last the stream was dammed up, and could not get on. Its course was choked by the rock, and by the dam made by the mud and sticks.

But the stream could not stay still. It rose and it rose, till it reached the top of the dam. Then, with a great roar, it burst on its way, and rushed on each side, all down the vale.

There was a great flood. All the live things that were in the vale were forced to flee for their lives. But it was no use. They had not time, and they all lost their lives in the flood.

That day the Hare was once more on the top of the hill. His eyes filled with tears when he saw the flood. "Poor things! poor things!" he said; "I can not bear the sight. How sad this loss of life is! It breaks my heart to see it. There is

C

but one thing that seems good to me at this sad time, and that is that I had to do with it in no way. I should die of grief, if, through my fault, such pain and woe came on the world!"

VII.—"*That is My Place.*"

N an old yew tree lived a Wren. She had built her nest there for two years, on the same bough. The third year, when she came to build her nest, she saw a young Wren on what she called her bough.

"What are you here for?" she said, for she saw that the young Wren had some moss in her beak, as if she meant to build her nest.

"I am here to build my nest," said the young Wren, in a pert voice.

"You must not, that is my place," said the old Wren.

"It is not. It is mine," cried the young one. "I was here first this spring. You are but just come, and see what I have done," and she showed some moss twined in the twigs of the bough.

"I don't care. It is my place," said the old Wren. "I had this tree first. I have had it two years, and now, when I come back, I find you here."

"First come, first served," said the young Wren.

"That is what I say," cried the old Wren, in a great rage.

"And that is what I say," said the young one. "So it is all right."

The old Wren gave the young one a peck, and tried to tear the moss off the twigs. The young one flew at her, and they had a great fight. Each cried out, "It is my place." "No, it is mine." "I was here first." "No, I was."

"What is all this?" said an old Cat, who lay near in the sun. "What a noise! I must go and see." So she went, and she heard what the two birds said.

They were in far too much of a rage to see her.

:"THAT IS MY PLACE."

But all at once they heard a great fierce voice close to them, which said, "You can not both have the place." And she caught them, each in one of her front paws. "It is not yours," she said to the old Wren. "You were too late this year. You are a cross bird, and you fight. I can not let you live."

And she ate her up.

"And it is not yours," she said to the young one. "The old Wren had it last year, you know. You have not been at all fair. I can not let you live."

So she ate her up too.

Then the Cat went down the tree, and lay in the sun.

"There is an end of that," said she.

VIII.—"*What is that to You?*"

THERE was once a Mule, who lived in a large field. In the next field lived a Horse, and a Cow, and a young Calf. The Mule was a cross, bad Mule, and the Cow had told the Calf not to talk to him. But the Calf would go, day by day, to the side of the hedge, and talk to him all the same.

Now in the Mule's field there was a pump.

One day the Calf came to the side of the hedge, and said to the Mule, "What is the name of that great thing in your field?"

Now to tell the truth, the Mule did not know, but he did not like to say so. So he said in a loud

fierce voice, "What is that to you?" The Calf
was young, and did not know much yet. She
thought that "What is that to you?" was the
name of the pump.

"It is a long grand name," she thought.

"The Horse and the Cow do not know that, I
am sure. I will show off to them how wise I
am."

So she said "What-is-that-to-you" nine or ten
times, till she could say it quite fast and well, all
in one word, and then she went up to the Horse
and said, with her head high in the air,

"Do you know the name of that thing in the
Mule's field?"

"No," said the Horse. "I should like to
know." He was not proud and vain, like the
Calf. "Do you know?" he asked.

"Yes," said the Calf, with her head still high
in the air. "Oh yes! I know quite well."

"What is it then?" said the Horse.

"What-is-that-to-you!" said the Calf, with a
grand air.

"Take that, you rude thing!" said the Horse,
and he gave her such a kick that she fell down,
and was much hurt.

The rest of the day she did not hold her head
high at all.

"It was all the fault of the Mule," she said.

IX.—" *I won't be put on.*"

WON'T be put on," said a young Horse, who had just been brought off the moor, where he had run wild all his life.

"Who wants to put on you?" asked an old Mare.

"Why, those men. They have put shoes on my feet!"

"A good thing, too," said the Mare.

"A good thing! Shoes on me! A free horse of the moor! as if I would wear these things!" And in a rage he kicked his feet on the stones, till at last he got off first one shoe, and then one more. "There!" he said. "I wear shoes! No, not I!"

Just then the Groom came in. He took the young Horse and the Mare, and put them both in

a break, that he might teach the young Horse how
to go.

The Horse reared when he felt the bit and the
curb, but it was of no use.

"When he cracks the whip," said the old Mare,
" he means that we must go fast."

"Oh, he does, does he?" said the Horse.
"Then he may crack for me! I won't be put on
in that way, I can tell him!"

And when the Groom cracked his whip, the
Horse would not go on, but stood quite still.

"This won't do," said the Groom, and he lashed
the Horse so hard that he soon did go on. He
did not play that trick twice.

"Oh! my fore feet hurt me so," said the Horse,
at last. "The stones cut them, and the hard road
makes them quite sore. Are yours sore?"

"No," said the Mare. "I have shoes on, you
know."

The Horse said no more, but he was glad to
get home. The Groom put him in a stall, and
put a thick cloth on him.

"What's that for?" said the Horse. "Just like that Man! When I am so hot that I do not know what to do, he puts this great thick thing on me. I won't be put on in that way." And he kicked till the cloth fell off.

But soon he felt cold. He got a chill, and all through the night he felt ill, and could not sleep for cold and pain. His feet were sore, and his sides were stiff.

"I wish I had that cloth on," he said. "I wish I had not kicked my shoes off. I wish I had gone on when the man cracked the whip. If he will but get me some more shoes, and let me have the cloth on, I will not say next time, 'I won't be put on.'"

X.—"He Did It First."

HERE were once two Sheep who lived in a field. One was black, and one was white. In the same field lived a Horse and a Cow.

Now the black Sheep was not at all good. But where he chose to go, the white Sheep would go, and what he did the white Sheep would do. So they both did what they ought not. And when the white Sheep was asked why he did what he ought not, he would say, "The black Sheep did it first!"

One day a Boy went through the field, and did not shut the gate. The black Sheep saw it, and ran out of the field with great glee. The white Sheep saw it too, and they both went some way.

But soon they met a large Dog, who knew that they ought not to be out in the road. He ran at them, and bit them, and tore some wool off their backs. They were glad to run back, and the white Sheep was quite ill with fright all the rest of the day.

" But why did you go ?" said the old Cow.

" The black Sheep went," said the white one. " He did it first."

Well, the gate was shut, but one day the black Sheep found a way out of the field through a hole in the hedge. He crept through the gap, and of course the white Sheep crept through it as well. They got out on the moor, and went a long way. They thought it fine fun to be out there, with no one in sight.

Soon the black Sheep, who was first, came to the edge of a deep pit. He gave a great jump and leaped in.

The white Sheep did nct stop to think. He gave a great jump, and leaped in too. Down, down, down he fell, on to a heap of great stones.

Both he and the black Sheep were much hurt. They could not get out, and were forced to lie there in great pain.

By-and-bye some Men came by, and saw the Sheep in the pit. The Men got them out, and took them back to the field, and sent for some one to see what could be done for them.

The Horse and the Cow, in great grief, came and stood by the side of the white Sheep as he lay on the grass. They were fond of him, in spite of all his faults.

"Oh! why," cried the Cow, with tears in her eyes (and the bell that was hung round her neck shook and rang as she leant over him)—"Why did you leave the field with the black Sheep?"

"He did it first," said the white one, in a faint voice.

"Then why did you jump down that steep place? Could you not see that it was a pit?"

"I did not stop to see. He did it first," said the white Sheep. Then, with a groan, he went on to ask, "How is the black Sheep? Is he here too? And what does the Man think who comes to see us?"

"I grieve to say," said the Cow, "that he thought you were both far too much hurt to live. The poor black Sheep, who lies close by, has just died, and I fear that you must die too."

"He did it first!" said the white Sheep. And with those words he died.

XI.—"*I Want to See the World.*"

THERE was once a young Pig, who wished to see the world. He lived in a sty with an old Sow, and he used to talk to her of his great plans, and of what he would do by-and-bye when he went out in the world. He had been born in the sty, and the door was too high for him to see the yard.

One day the farm boy did not shut the door of the sty.

"Ho! ho! now is my time!" cried the Pig. "Now I'm off! It is no good for you to come, you poor old thing," he said to the Sow. "You would be in my way, and in your own as well, for I know you do not care to see the world. I will come back and let you have a look at me when I am a great Pig."

"I WANT TO SEE THE WORLD."

"Take care, take care," said the old Sow. "It may be well to go out in the world, if you must, but it is best to stop at home if you can."

"Poor old thing!" was all the young Pig said, and he turned up his snout as he said it.

He went through the door, out in the yard. It was a square yard, with a high wall all round it, and a high door in one side of the wall.

"So this is the world," said he, "What a large place it is! Dear me! I must take care, or I shall be lost. I must keep close by the edge of the world, so that I may not lose my way."

So he walked on by the side of the wall, and soon saw a flock of Geese. They put out their heads and made a great noise as he went by. The young Pig did not like this, and he went on as fast as he could. But as soon as he had passed, he felt quite proud that he had seen such strange things.

Next he saw two Ducks in a pond, who cried, "Quack! quack!" when they saw him.

"What does that mean?" thought the Pig. But

he could not find out. "How much I shall have to tell when I get home!" he thought.

By this time he had got to the high door.

"This must be the end of the world," said he, for he could not see through.

He went on, still by the side of the wall, and met a large Cow, and when he saw her great horns, he thought he had best get out of her way as fast as he could. So he made haste, and soon found that he was back at the door of his own sty.

"So here you are!" said the old Sow.

"Here I am!" cried the Pig.

"And what have you seen?"

"Oh! such things! I have been all round the world. I find that it is square, and has a wall all round it, lest pigs should fall off. In fact, it is like a big sty."

"Well, to be sure!" said the old Sow.

"And the end of the world," went on the young Pig, "is made of wood, and has two high posts, one on each side, to mark the place. The first thing that I saw in the world was a herd of such queer pigs. They had but two legs each, and they were quite white. Then I saw two pigs that could swim. There are but two in the world. Think of that! And they said, " Quack! quack!"

"What does that mean?" asked the old Sow.

"Oh! it is what they say in the world," said the young Pig, with a grand air. "It is no good to tell you what it means, for you have not been there, you know. Then I saw a huge red pig with two horns. There is but one pig of this sort in the whole world!"

"Well, to be sure!" said the old Sow.

"I should have made friends with him," went on the young Pig, "but he did not look my way. And then, as I had gone all round the world, I came home. Ah! the world is a fine place, you poor old thing!" and he turned up his snout once more.

"I know all that is to be known now," said he. "The farm boy may shut the door when he likes. I am a great Pig now. I know the world!"

"Well, to be sure!" said the old Sow.

XII.—*"I Don't Know."*

HERE was once a young Rat who would not take the pains to make up his mind. When the old Rats asked him if he would like to come out with them at night, he would say, " I don't know ;" and if they said, "Would you like to stay in?" he still used the same words, " I don't know." He would not take the pains to make a choice, or to find out which he would like.

An old grey Rat said to him one day—

" No one will care for you, if you go on like this. You have no more mind than a blade of grass. It is good to give up your own way, but it is not good to have no way at all."

The young Rat sat up, and looked wise, but said not a word.

" Don't you think so?" said the old grey Rat,

and he gave a stamp with his hind feet, for he could not bear to see the young one so cool.

"I don't know," was all the young Rat said, and then he walked off with slow steps, to think for an hour if he should stay at home in the hole, or go out in the loft.

One day there was a great noise in the loft. It was old, and the rain had soaked through some of the beams, so that the place was not safe to live in. On this day one of the joists gave way, and a beam fell with one end on the floor. The walls shook, and the hair of all the rats stood on end with fright.

"This will not do," said the old Rats, and they shook their heads as they spoke. "We must leave this place."

So they sent out scouts to look for a new home, and in the night the scouts came back, and said they had found an old barn, where there would be room and food for all.

"Then it is best to go at once," said the old Rat, who was the chief. "Form in line."

The Rats came forth from their holes, and stood on the floor in a long line.

"Are all here?" and the old grey Rat looked round. "You all choose to go?" asked he. "Make up your minds at once."

"Yes, yes," said all in the line.

Just then the chief caught sight of young Grip (that was the young Rat's name). He was not in the line, nor was he out : he stood just by it.

"You did not speak, Grip," he said ; "of course you will come?"

"I don't know," said Grip.

"Don't know! Why, you do not think it safe, do you?"

"I don't know," said Grip. "The roof may not come down yet."

"Well, stay then," said the old Rat, "and serve you right if you are killed."

"I don't know that I will stay," said Grip. "The roof might come down soon."

"Well, we can not wait for you to make up

your mind. Come or stay, as you like. Right face, Rats! March!"

And the long line marched out of the loft. Down the steps they went, one by one, and the young Rat looked on.

"I think I will go," he said; "but yet—I don't know. It is nice and snug here."

The tail of the last Rat was lost to sight as he spoke. He went near the steps, and looked down. "I will go back to my hole for a short time, just to make up my mind," said he.

That night there was a great crash. Down came beams, joists, tiles, and the whole roof.

The next day some men came to look at the loft. They thought it odd to see no Rats, but at last, as one man moved a great tile, he saw a young Rat, quite dead, half in and half out of his hole.

XIII.—"*Why?*"

OU must not go in there?" said an old Dog to a young Pup, who stood on the white steps of a large house. "You must stay out now."

"Why?" asked the young Pup. For it was a trick (and a bad trick) of his to say "Why?" when he was told to do, or not to do, a thing.

"Why?" said the old Dog. "I can not say why. Old as I am, I do not know why. But I do know that if you go in, when it is a wet day like this, the Maid will drive you out."

"But why?" went on the Pup. "It is not fair. There is no sense in it. I have been in the house some days, and no one turned me out, so why should they now?"

"WHY?"

" Those were fine days," said the old Dog.

" Well, it is the wet days that I most want to be in," said the Pup. " And I don't see why I should stay out. So here I go."

And so he did.

But he soon found that though no one stopped to tell him " why " he must not come in, it was quite true that he might not.

The first who saw him was the Cook, who had a broom in her hand.

" That vile pup ! " she cried. " Look at his feet ! "

" What is wrong with my feet?" barked the Pup.

But she did not wait to tell him. She struck him with the broom, and he fled with a howl up the stairs.

" Oh, that Pup ! " cried the Maid, as she saw the marks of his feet. " He ought not to come in the house at all, if he will not keep out on wet days."

" But why ? " yelped the Pup, as the Maid threw a hearth brush at his head.

Still no one told him why. But a Man just then came up stairs.

"Why, what a mess!" he said. "Oh, I see. It is that Pup. I thought he knew he must not come in."

"So I did, but I did not know why," growled the Pup, as with sore back and lame foot, he crept under a chair.

"Come out, come out," cried the Man. "I will not have you in the house at all. Out with you!" And he seized him with a strong hand, and chained him up in a stall.

"You might have stopped out, and played on the grass, if you had stayed there," he said. "But as you will come in the house when you ought not, you must be kept where you can not do so."

And so the young Pup had to stay in the dull stall. And when at last he was let out, he did not ask "Why?" if he was told to do, or not to do, a thing, but did as he ought at once, like a wise dog.

XIV.—" *You Daren't.*"

"YOU can't jump that," said a Goat to a Sheep.

They were on a cliff near the sea. In the cliff there was a deep, deep cleft or crack, which went down to the sea. It was not broad, but it was too wide for a Goat or a Sheep to cross. At high tide the waves of the sea foamed and raged in this cleft, and it was high tide now.

The Goat and the Sheep stood on one side of the cleft.

The Sheep looked, but said not a word. She knew it was too much of a jump for her, but she was too vain to say so.

"You daren't," said the Goat.

The Sheep did not like this. She would not say it was true that she dared not, and she did not know what else to say. At last she thought of a way out.

E

"You daren't!" said she.

Now it was the Goat's turn to look vexed.

"You just say that to get out of it!" he cried. "You daren't, you know."

"You daren't, you know," said the Sheep.

"I do dare, then!" cried the Goat.

"So do I," said the Sheep. "How dare you say I don't dare?"

"You don't!" cried the Goat.

"You don't!" cried the Sheep.

"I do! I do!" cried both at the same time.

And at the same time both, as if with one voice, cried, "Prove it!"

There was a pause. Both went back a few steps, ran to the edge of the cleft, and leapt with all their might.

It was too wide. The Sheep fell in the midst of the cleft. The Goat just touched the edge of the side with his foot, but could not gain sure hold, and he fell too.

When the tide turned, a dead Goat and a dead Sheep were swept out to sea.

XV.—*"I am as Good as You."*

ONCE there was a Cat, whose name was Smut. But she chose to say it was Grim, for she thought that was a grand name. She liked to be thought much of, and to say to all she met, "I am as good as you."

One day she set out to see what could be seen in the world.

First she came to a sty, in which was a great, fat Pig. She leapt up on the wall, and said, "Good day, Pig."

"Who are you?" said the Pig.

"I? I am as good as you, I hope," cried the Cat.

"No doubt," said the Pig, for he was not proud. And he was glad to find some one who would talk to him.

The Cat was well pleased. "This Pig is a wise

Pig," thought she. "He knows what is what, I can see." So she sat on the wall, and told him all the news.

Then she went on, and met a Dog in the yard.

"What do you want here?" said he, in a gruff voice.

"You are here," cried the Cat. "And I am as good as you, I hope."

"Humph!" said the Dog.

"He is not half as nice as the Pig," thought the Cat. And she said, "I can not stay. It will be dark soon, and I must find a house to sleep in. Good day, Dog."

"Humph!" said the Dog.

She went on some way, and came to what she thought was a house. She went in, and saw a Horse in a stall. He was blind, but he heard her come in, and he said, "Who is there?"

"It is I," said the Cat, in as loud a voice as she could.

"What an odd voice," thought the Horse. And he said, "But who are you?"

"I am as good as you," said the Cat.

"Are you a Horse?"

"Well, I am not quite a Horse," said the Cat. "But I am as good as one."

"What is your name?" said the Horse.

"My name is the great Grim."

"And how tall are you? For I can not see, you know."

"My head is as high as the top of the door," said the Cat. And, in fact, so it was, for she had got up on to the top of the door, where there was a nice broad ledge for her to sit on.

"How grand you must be!" said the Horse. "Will you share my stall, if you have no place to sleep in?"

"Thank you," said the Cat, "You are most kind. If you will take care to leave room for me, I will come when it gets dark. But mind you leave room for me."

"I will," said the Horse, and he went quite on one side of the stall.

In the night the Cat came, and lay down on the

straw.   There she went to sleep.   The Horse had
not gone to sleep, but he did not hear her come
in.

"Why does not the great Grim come?" thought
he.   "I will let him have this side of the stall, I
think.   It is not so cold as the side near the
door."

So he went to the side by the door.   As he did
so, he trod on the Cat's tail.

"Mew!" cried she.

"Why, what can that be?" said he.   "You
must move out of the way, if you please."   But as
he spoke, he put his hoof on the Cat's head.
There was one loud "Mew!"   Then all was still.

Next day the Horse heard the Groom come to
the door, and say to a Boy, who was with him,
"Why! there is a dead Cat in the stall!"

"Poor thing!" thought the Horse.   "But
where can the great Grim be?"

XVI.—*"That's Nought to Me."*

———————◆———————

 DOG once set out to go through the world and see all that was to be seen. He had been spoilt in his young days, and his heart was hard, so he did not care for the pains or the joys of those that he saw, as long as he was safe and pleased. In this way he lost half the joys that he might have had, and was of none of the use that he might have been, but he did not know that, or, if he did know, he did not care.

One day as he went through a field he heard a sad cry, and when he looked round he saw a Sheep in a stream.

"Help me! oh, help me!" she cried; "I shall be drowned."

The Dog could have pulled her out, for he was a

strong Dog, and could swim well; but he said in a calm voice, "That is nought to me," and went on.

The Sheep was not drowned, for the stream took her down to a place where the bank was low, and she could get out; but she owed the Dog no thanks for that.

He went on, till he thought he must find some food, and just then he caught sight of a Cat, in the yard of a house near by. The Cat had a pan of milk, which she seemed to like, for she purred as she lapped at it.

"Hi there!" cried the Dog; "give me some of your milk."

The Cat arched her back, and growled, but said not a word. She thought the Dog would not come in; but he did, and drove her from the pan with a snarl which showed his great teeth.

"Oh, do not take it all, pray!" cried the Cat, "it is all I shall have; I do not have milk more than once in a day."

"I don't care. That is nought to me," said the

"THAT'S NOUGHT TO ME."

Dog; and he drank it all up, and went on, well pleased.

Day after day he was the same. He would not help a poor Cow that had got shut out of her field though he knew of a gap in the hedge by which she could have got back. He would not take the pains to point out the way to the old oak in the wood, when a young Bird, who had strayed too far from its nest, asked him. To each and all he said, " It is nought to me."

At last he came to a great wood. He was tired, and not quite well too, for he had found a large piece of meat, all of which he ate at one meal. So he thought he must rest for a time, though he had heard it was not a safe place to sleep in, for there were said to be wolves there.

And soon he went to sleep.

In his sleep he dreamed that, all at once, a great Wolf came out of the wood and seized hold of him.

" Save me! save me!" he cried.

"Why should I save you?" said the Wolf, with

a fierce gleam in his eye. "Is there one who would say a good word for you?"

At this speech the Sheep, who had asked the Dog to help her, came out of the wood.

"I have a word to say," she said, in a grave voice, "but it is not a good word. This Dog would not help me. 'It is nought to me' if you kill him."

"Oh!" groaned the poor Dog. "Is there none who will say a kind word?"

Then came the Cat. "I do not care if you kill him," she said to the Wolf. "'It is nought to me.' He did not care for my grief."

The Cow came next. "Do as you like," she said. "He is no good. 'It is nought to me' what is done with such as he."

And then came a whole crowd of Beasts and Birds, and they stood round and cried, with one voice, "Do as you will with him. 'It is nought to us.'"

The Dog's fear in his dream was so great that he woke. How great was his joy to find that no Wolf was near!

"But it might have been true!" he thought. "I will mend my ways. I will not go through the world as I have done; and I will not say of those who live in the same world with me that their joy, or grief, or pain is 'Nought to me!'"

XVII.—"*More, More.*"

JICK and Jock were two young Rooks, who lived at the top of a tall tree in a copse. They were quite young, and could not get their own food yet, but though they were the same age, they were not the same in some things.

When the old birds brought food to the nest, Jick would not wait for his fair turn. He called out "More, more" when he had just had some, and as he was a fine young bird, and Jock was not, Jick was the pet of the old Rooks, and so got more than was good for him, while poor Jock got less. All the fat worms, and slugs, fell to Jick's share, so day by day he grew more fat, and called out still, "More, more."

Jock soon found that he should not be well off

till he could get his own food. So he tried to hop and fly soon, and went through all the drill that old Rooks teach their young ones, and most of the Rooks in the copse said he got on well, and were grieved to see him so lean and thin. But Jick, who had all done for him, did not care to find food, or to fly. He grew so fat that he lay all day in the nest, and blinked his eyes.

"You spoil that child!" said all the wise Rooks to those who brought Jick food. " He will be the worse for it, you will see."

"O no! the pet!" they said. "When he asks in that sweet way for ' More, more!' we must give it him."

So things went on, and all the young Rooks could get their own food but Jick.

One day the old ones brought him a large worm.

"That will make you a good meal," they said, "and be quick, for we hear some boys are near, with their guns, and we want to be off."

Jick was quick, but as soon as the worm was

gone, he gaped with his great beak, and cried, " More, more."

" One might have done for you," said the old ones, " but what must be, must." And off they flew to find more food.

Once, twice, thrice, did they bring him " one more" worm, and then Jick, too fat and sick to eat more, shut his eyes, and went to sleep.

" Bang! bang!" went a gun. Two shots were fired, and the two old birds fell dead. But Jick did not know. Jock knew, and he, the one for whom they did not care, was the one who mourned when they fell.

" Wake! wake!" he cried to Jick. But Jick did not wake.

" Wake!" cried Jock once more. " Here is a boy at the foot of the tree. He will climb up. Wake, and fly."

But Jick still did not wake.

The boy did climb, and Jock, when he drew near, gave Jick a great peck to wake him up, and then flew to a bough near by.

"There is one on that bough," cried the boy to a man who had the gun. "Don't shoot him, though, he is too lean."

"Could not shoot him if he was not," said the man, "he is out of reach." For Jock, when he heard the boy speak, had spread his wings, and flown off with ease.

"Why do you go on?" cried the man to the boy. "It is too late in the year to find young Rooks in the nest."

"Is it, though?" asked the boy. "Here is a fat one. Why, he can't fly, I do think."

Jick woke now. He stood on his feet, and tried to fly, but he could not. He was so fat and dull, and blinked so with his eyes, that the boy laughed.

"You might as well have hopped into my hand as have sat here," he said.

"Save me, save me," the Rook tried to say, but the words that came were, "More, more." The boy did not know what they meant, though.

So the two old ones and Jick were baked in the same pie.

F

XVIII.—*"It is Too Hard."*

"YOU must learn to fly," said a white Dove to her two young ones, as they sat in the nest.

"I'll try," said Pluff, who was a good Dove.

"Oh, I can't, it is too hard," said Duff.

"Now, do as I do," said the old Dove. "I will take care of you. Hop on this bough. Spread your wings like me, and fly to this branch quite near."

Pluff tried. His heart beat, and his head swam. when he found himself first in the air, but he tried to do just as he was told, and in a short time (which seemed to him, though, a long time), he found that he was safe on the branch.

But Duff was not there. He still sat in the nest.

"Come, Duff," cried the old Dove. "You must come. If you do not learn to fly, you will die. You will starve, for I shall not feed you when you get big. And if a storm comes, and blows down the nest, you will be killed if you can not fly."

"IT IS TOO HARD."

"Oh, I can not," said Duff; "it is too hard."

"Why, Pluff has done it, and what Pluff has done, you can do. Come, hop on this bough. I will have it done."

So Duff hopped on the bough. But he would not spread his wings. He would not trust to what he was told. He slunk back to the nest, and there he stayed.

Day by day it was the same. And when Pluff could fly quite well, Duff could not fly at all. He had not once tried.

One night a storm came. The tree in which the nest was, rocked to and fro. The nest was old, and at last it gave way. The old Dove and Pluff flew out as it fell, and were not hurt, but Duff, what of him?

They cried to him to spread his wings; but he could not fly.

"It is too hard," he moaned as he fell on the hard ground.

And so it was. He was killed by the fall.

XIX.—"*Why Not?*"

HERE was once a young Sprat, who lived in the sea. One day, as he swam by the shore, he saw a small stream, which ran down to the sea through the sand.

"I think I shall go up there when the tide is high," said he.

"Up where!" asked a Sole, who heard him.

"Up that stream, to be sure! Do you see how nice it looks? No rough waves or great rocks to bruise my smooth sides, and rub my bright scales. Yes! I shall go up there at high tide."

"Pray don't think of such a thing!" said the Sole, with a grave face. "The stream is not meant for you; your place is in the sea, and in the sea you should stay."

"But I don't want to stay," said the young Fish,

with a cross flap of his tail; "there are fish in the stream, I know, and why should not I be there?"

"The stream is fresh," said the Sole, "and the sea is salt. If you tried to live in the stream, you would die. Some sorts of fish are meant for the sea, and some for the stream. You are meant to live in the sea, and it is no good for you to fret."

"I shall fret! I will fret!" said the Sprat; "that is, if I do not go. But I will go—so there!"

"Take your own way, then."

"And as to what you say of the kinds of fish," cried the young Fish, "I know that the same sorts do live in the sea and in the streams, or ponds, which are the same, of course. Crabs, and Shrimps, and Flat Fish live in both, I know; and why not I?"

"Why not? I am sick of your 'Why not's,'" said the Sole. "The same Crab or Shrimp could not live in the sea and in the stream. They are not the same sort."

"Well, then!" said the young Fish, "I know there is one sort that does live both in the sea and

in the streams—I have seen some. They go up
the streams, and stay there, and then come back.
I know it. And they get so fat and big, and splash
and dash about in the streams, and have such fun."

"THEY do! yes! But you are not one of them.
You can not do what they do." And the Sole
looked with a smile on the small Sprat by his
side.

"I don't see why not," said the Sprat. "You
can stay here, old Stick-in-the-Sand! but I shall
not." And he swam off.

He went to a shoal of Sprats and told them
what was in his mind. They all joined fins, and
said they would do what no Sprat yet had done.
"If some fish can do it, why not all?" said our
young friend.

And all said, "Why not?"

One Sprat, who thought he was a great wit,
made a verse, which they all sang as they set forth
for the stream. It ran thus—

"If some fish can, why not all?
    If the great, why not the small?"

But the old Sole, who met them on their way, said they ought to add this third line—
"Pride, they say, must have a fall."
which they did not like to hear.

By help of the high tide, they got some way up the stream. They were in high glee, and laughed, and flapped their tails.

"This is grand!" they cried. "We shall soon grow big and fat, and splash, and dash, and leap in the fresh stream."

But soon the tide began to slack. They got to a small hole in the stream, and lay there. The salt tide passed back down the stream.

"Ugh! how vile this stream tastes!" said one. "Is this what they call fresh?"

"Ah! I feel sick—so sick!" cried our friend. "I shall die. I can not live in this. It is not like the sea. Let us go back."

"Let us go back!" they all cried. But when they tried, they found they had got so far up the stream, and were in so deep a hole, that it was hard work to get back.

"Oh! the sea! the dear old sea!" they said. "Shall we get back there? We feel as if we should die in this stream. It makes us so weak and ill."

It did make them ill. They gasped, and their bright skins looked dull and pale. Their fins seemed to have no strength, and some of the poor Sprats gave up at last, turned on their sides, and died in the stream. Some got back, and they reached the sea with great pains, but they did not look like the same which had set out a few hours since. The old fish were kind to them, and did not laugh or scorn them. They could see at a glance what the poor things had gone through, but they used for a long time to tell the tale of the Sprats to any young fish who was heard to say "Why not?"

XX.—"*Those Old Folks.*"

"I DON'T see why we should make our cells the same way as they have been made till now," said a young Queen Bee to the crowd round her. "Those Old Folks will have them with six sides. And why, pray? Let us try a new plan. We will have them round."

"Yes, yes," cried the bees with one voice, for they had just been put into a new hive, and could do as they liked. "Those old folks! We will see what we can do."

So they tried round cells, but soon found it was a great waste of room and of wax to make them. Then they tried square, but found the walls would not bear the weight when they were full. Then they tried two or three shapes at the same time, and made them fit as they could, but that gave them much more work, and was no use.

Time went on all the same, and their heads were so full of their own plans, and of scorn for 'those old folks,' and they tried such odd ways, that at last no one knew what the old shape had been.

" Let us try cells with six sides," said a young Bee one day, when they had tried all the ways they could.

" Six sides! ah, yes!" said the Queen. " What a bright thought."

So they pulled down the old cells and built them up with six sides.   They were just right!

" There," cried they all with great joy, " see what we have found out!   This is the best way that could be!   If 'those old folks' could but see us now, and our new plans!"

And those Bees still jeer at " those old folks!"

Turnbull & Spears, Printers.

M.—11/82.—S

Lightning Source UK Ltd.
Milton Keynes UK
UKHW051016150223
416722UK00028B/494